# Holiness To the LORD

## Biblical Standards of Modesty

Jason DeMars

ISBN-13: 978-1-9808-5031-1
Imprint: Independently published

# CONTENTS

# PREFACE

This book was originally written to be translated into Farsi and act as a biblical explanation of modesty and holiness for the new or confused believers in Iran and Turkey. I began to preach upon the subject in various churches in the United States and several sisters and brothers spoke with me or emailed me saying that questions they had for many years about this subject had been answered.

Therefore, *Holiness to the Lord* is intended to examine the basic "ABC's" of the Message that God gave to Brother William Marrion Branham. Those that have been raised in the Message generally understand hair, make-up and dress. However, very often, the scriptural and historical details about *why* this is so, are an unknown. They simply know that Brother Branham said so and the basic scriptural and historical proofs that he offered. Our purpose is not to pretend that we are exalted above anyone else. However, Brother Branham made this marvelous statement that I take to heart:

"There is two systems working in the church world today. I'm going to get this off my shoulder, and then I have it over with. We all know that that's the Word of God, and the denominational system. There is the two systems at work. Just as they was, Jacob and Esau; one after the Spirit, the other one after the flesh. And what is it? Esau and Jacob was fighting in the wombs of the mother, even to the time they were born. And so is the denominational and the Word, fighting, one against the other. They have been, since Luther first brought the first reformation. I hope that's simple enough that you can understand it. See? These men, if they pick up This and goes out with It, they can make more sense to It, see, to bring It to a place you would. I just want to lay this Seed, then hope they make It come to Life. Notice. See?" [1]

We can see here that it is the duty of the five-fold ministry of Ephesians 4:11 to "make more sense to it" [the Message] and "make it come to life." This is my purpose in writing this book. The seed has been laid down; now we want to study closely, to make more sense of it. It is not that we make another sense to it because it already makes sense, but we want to clarify: that is, to place it scripturally. The duty and work of an apostle is "to set the things in order" [2] and the teacher is to "take the Words and put them together by the Holy Spirit." [3] This is the purpose and the calling that the Lord has led me to. I write that, not with pride, but with humility of heart, knowing that makes me the servant of all. The duty of leaders is to feed the flock of God and not to exercise lordship over them. My purpose is to be faithful to the scriptures and the revelation of them that were brought to us through the ministry that came in fulfillment of Malachi 4:5-6. God's clear pattern is laid out marvelously in the "Seven Church Ages" book.

"In every age we have exactly the same pattern. That is why the light comes through some God-given messenger in a certain area, and then from that messenger there spreads the light through the ministry of others who have been faithfully taught. But of course all those who go out don't always learn how necessary it

[1] 65-0124, Birth Pain, Rev. William Marrion Branham
http://table.branham.org

[2] 63-0724, God Doesn't Call Man To Judgment Without First Warning Him, Rev. William Marrion Branham
http://table.branham.org

[3] 63-0724, God Doesn't Call Man To Judgment Without First Warning Him, Rev. William Marrion Branham
http://table.branham.org

is to speak ONLY what the messenger has spoken. (Remember, Paul warned the people to say only what he said, I Corinthians 14:37, "If any man think himself to be a prophet or spiritual, let him acknowledge that the things that I write unto you are the COMMANDMENTS OF THE LORD. What? came the Word of God out from you? or came it unto you only?") They add here, or take away there, and soon the Message is no longer pure, and the revival dies down. How careful we must be to hear ONE voice, for the Spirit has but one voice which is the voice of God. Paul warned them to say what he said, even as Peter did likewise. He warned them that EVEN HE (PAUL) could not change one word of what he had given by revelation. Oh, how important it is to hear the voice of God by way of His messengers, and then say what has been given them to say to the churches." [4]

As we study upon this subject it is my purpose to be faithful to what has already been delivered by the Lord through his messenger. But, even as the messenger spoke, it is my purpose to make more sense of it by examining things with a microscope and to fill in any gaps that might be there in your understanding using the scripture and history. I have never viewed myself as the only pebble on the beach, but I am one pebble, nonetheless and I aim to do my part to encourage your faith.

---

[4] An Exposition Of The Seven Church Ages - Chapter Four - The Smyrnaean Church Age, Rev. William Marrion Branham
http://table.branham.org

# Chapter 1

# HOLINESS OF THE PRIESTHOOD

## Kings and Priests

"You shall make a plate of pure gold and engrave on it, like the engraving of a signet, Holy to the Lord." (Exodus 28:36)

In any writing on modesty and holiness, we must first start with the work of God in the lives of believers according to the scripture. When we are saved this results in a work of renewal and transformation in our lives. Let's examine some principles given to us from the Old Testament and the New.

The high priest was to wear a plate that was engraved with the phrase: "Holy to the LORD." Not only was he to merely wear something which expressed "Holy to the LORD," this was to be an outward expression of what his life was. The high priest was set aside for God's purpose. To be holy means to be separate, it means to be different than others. It is not being different or separate solely for the sake of being different or separate. It was to be separate and different to the LORD.

Our separation from the world is according to the purpose of God and for his glory. The high priest had specific requirements for his clothes, hair and behavior. But it is not just the high priest that needed to be holy. In the Psalms, David writes that all the saints should worship the LORD in the beauty of holiness:

"Ascribe to the Lord the glory due his name; worship the Lord in the splendor of holiness." (Psalms 29:2)

## Believers are Kings and Priests Holy Before God

Every believer is called to be separated and to be different from the world. The high priest was to be separated unto God both externally and internally. That is, his clothing was different, but so was his behavior. It is clear according to the Word that our behavior starts from our heart.

"And he said, 'What comes out of a person is what defiles him. For from within, out of the heart of man, come evil thoughts, sexual immorality, theft, murder, adultery, coveting, wickedness, deceit, sensuality, envy, slander, pride, foolishness. All these evil things come from within, and they defile a person.'" (Mark 7:20-23)

So, these wicked behaviors which Christ condemns start from the heart. By implication we know that the opposite is true as well. Holy behavior starts from the heart. The problem is that we are born with an evil heart.

"The heart is deceitful above all things, and desperately wicked: who can know it?" (Jeremiah 17:9)

We are born with the nature to sin, therefore we choose sin. For godly behavior to come forth, that desperately wicked heart must be transformed. It is through the Gospel of Jesus Christ that we receive a new heart.

"I want to point out succinctly, that we are saved by grace through faith and not of works. Our behavior does not affect our salvation. We are not saved by having good behavior. We are saved by the sacrificial death of Jesus Christ on the cross. We receive that salvation by faith apart from works." (Ephesians 2:8-9).

"Yea, a man may say, Thou hast faith, and I have works: Shew me thy faith without thy works, and I will shew thee my faith by my works. Thou believest that there is one God; thou doest well: the devils also believe, and tremble. But wilt thou know, O vain man, that faith without works is dead?" (James 2:18-20)

As James writes, without works our faith is dead. Demons believe in one God, but that does not mean they have experienced salvation. We can believe in the fact of one God, the fact of the resurrection and the Lordship of Jesus, but how has that belief affected our lives? If our lives don't produce the fruit of good works and holiness, then it is clear that something is lacking to our faith.

Living holy is a reflection of His holiness. Yes, we are saved by grace, yet God is holy, and the Word of God brings a separating from unbelievers, a holiness set apart from the world.

Being saved from the wrath of God by the blood of Jesus Christ means we are born of the Spirit of God. But what does it mean to be born of the Spirit? When we are born of the Spirit we become new people (2 Corinthians 5:17). That means our nature changes. Before we had evil thoughts, committed adultery, lied, slandered people, used drugs, smoked and drank alcohol. Now our nature has changed.

When our nature changes, the things that we want to do change. We no longer want to drink, we no longer want to smoke, we no longer want to lie or steal or have sex outside of marriage. If your desires have not changed, it shows you need to receive the Holy Ghost. Ask the Father and he will give it to you. This is the way that God creates holiness in us. He changes our desires, and this results in our behavior changing.

## Sanctification

"But we ought always to give thanks to God for you, brothers beloved by the Lord, because God chose you as the first-fruits to be saved, through sanctification by the Spirit and belief in the truth." (2 Thessalonians 2:13)

Sanctification is without doubt linked to holiness and modesty. The word itself means: to make holy. And the Scripture above tells us that sanctification is done by the Spirit of God. This holiness is not a mere external thing that deals with outward appearances. Any external reformation done of our own power can easily be undone. But sanctification from God starts in our heart. He changes our nature and gives us new desires. He creates in us a desire for holiness, and that desire for holiness has its foundation in God.

## Joy of the Lord

"We cannot look at the true faith of the Bible as an outward form that we check off the list when we have fulfilled our duty. In fact, a church or group of people that are living without true joy and true peace are actually missing the mark. There are cults and dangerous groups of people that stifle any free thought and force their members to dress and speak a certain way. This is not the way of the Lord. God deals with our heart, gives us joy and peace (in the midst of great trials and pain) and transforms us to be more like Jesus Christ. There is no other religion on earth that tells its followers that they should be full of joy. Actually, the one true God that created heaven and earth created the human being to be happy. Because of sin we seek to find happiness in material things. "Delight yourself in the Lord, and he will give you the desires of your heart." (Psalms 37:4)

As believers in God, our first desire should be for him. In Psalm 63, we read that our greatest passion and desire should be for God. That is to have our flesh and our soul satisfied with His presence, with worshipping and living for Him. Ultimately, worship is not merely singing songs and praying, but our lives are surrendered to God and we are doing what he asks of us. Many times, these things find their expression in singing, lifting our hands and praising. However, sometimes it's found in serving someone in need. It is not a bad thing to feel joy when we do God's will. It should be our delight to follow after the plan of God for our lives. And this pleasure we experience flows from the presence of God.

"Then he said to them, 'Go your way. Eat the fat and drink sweet wine and send portions to anyone who has nothing ready, for this day is holy to our Lord. And do not be grieved, for the joy of the Lord is your strength.'" (Nehemiah 8:10)

When times are difficult and there are many struggles, we find that the joy of the Lord is indeed our strength. Being with God in prayer and worship brings such a satisfaction to our lives that we receive strength. Regardless of what the government does to us or what our family does to us, we can be strong because we have a relationship with Jesus Christ and we find joy in Him: "You make known to me the path of life; in your presence there is fullness of joy; at your right hand are pleasures forevermore." (Psalms 16:11)

Through the Bible and the Spirit of God the path of life is made known to us. That is, the commands that he has for us to follow are made known in scripture. And by following the Word of God, by grace we come into the presence of God, and we experience fullness of joy and pleasure for eternity.

When we obey the Word of God (the path of Life) from our heart, we experience joy. It is not legalism to obey the Word of God. We are not saved by our obedience, but we make genuine faith known by obeying the Word of God. And in obeying the Word of God we experience the joy of The Lord.

# Abiding in His Presence: Surrendering to His Commandments

"As the Father has loved me, so have I loved you. Abide in my love. If you keep my commandments, you will abide in my love, just as I have kept my Father's commandments and abide in his love. These things I have spoken to you, that my joy may be in you, and that your joy may be full." (John 15:9-11)

If we love Jesus, we will listen to what he says, and we'll do it. We won't treat what he says lightly or take it as an either/or option. We will take his Word to heart and obey it. In other religions, obedience is done as a duty. When you are obeying out of duty, joy is not present. In the Gospel of Jesus Christ, we obey because of our relationship. We obey because we love the Lord Jesus Christ. We obey because it is a delight. We obey because it makes us happy, and Jesus spoke his Word to us so that our joy would be full.

## God Restrains Our Behavior Under the Gospel

"Or do you not know that the unrighteous will not inherit the kingdom of God? Do not be deceived: neither the sexually immoral, nor idolaters, nor adulterers, nor men who practice homosexuality, nor thieves, nor the greedy, nor drunkards, nor revilers, nor swindlers will inherit the kingdom of God. And such were some of you. But you were washed, you were sanctified, you were justified in the name of the Lord Jesus Christ and by the Spirit of our God." (1 Corinthians 6:9-11)

There are certain behaviors that we are commanded not to do. If we do them, it demonstrates that we will not inherit the kingdom of God. People who are sexually immoral, worship false gods, commit adultery, are homosexuals, thieves, drunks, partiers, and those who commit extortion will not go to heaven. This behavior is sinful and shuts us out of the kingdom of God. We cannot say that God does not give us commands. It is not legalistic to tell people to not commit adultery or perform homosexual acts or to steal. Legalism is: following the commandments of men, to please men (who claim to stand in the place of God), not obedience to God out of a pure heart.

Notice that Paul goes directly to an inward work of God in your life. But you are washed, sanctified, and justified by the Spirit of God. This spiritual work of God through Christ affects our external behavior. If you are washed, justified and sanctified in the name of our Lord Jesus Christ then you will not commit these ungodly acts. You are not saved by not committing ungodly acts, rather the effect of salvation is deliverance from captivity to sin. By nature, we are born in bondage to sin and are under the dominion of Satan. Through the grace of God and the blood of Christ we are made free, given a new nature that leads us to obedience.

"Know ye not, that to whom ye yield yourselves servants to obey, his servants ye are to whom ye obey; whether of sin unto death, or of obedience unto righteousness?" (Romans 6:16)

With that said, there is a great error made by modern Christianity. A large portion of the Word of God has been left out, and people have been allowed to violate it freely. My intention is not to force you into any kind of behavior, but to point out what the plain teaching of scripture is. Then you can decide what you want to do. You decide if you want to obey or not. There is a true Christian identity. We must find God's standard of modesty.

## Chapter 2

# GOD COMMANDS MODESTY

"You have heard that it was said, 'You shall not commit adultery.' But I say to you that whoever looks at a woman with lustful intent has already committed adultery with her in his heart." (Matthew 5:27, 28)

God gives us commands not to be hard on us, but to protect us and guard us from evil. Sin is a violation of the nature of God. The moral law of God, given to us via the Ten Commandments and surrounding moral ordinances is an expression of the nature and character of God. Sin is a violation of the nature of God. When we receive a command, it is with the intent that we are to obey. When we walk in obedience to that command we are living as man was meant to live. When we disobey, we violate the very nature of the universe, and in so doing corrupt both our own innermost being itself.

When the Lord Jesus commands us not to even look at a woman lustfully it goes from our outward act, to our inward motive. Not only is our outward action sinful, but the motive within the heart is sinful. This is what leads to outward sin. Let's examine these words more closely. Since men are very visually oriented, they tend to be attracted to a woman physically very quickly. Satan preys upon men this way to cause them to lust. Jesus states that a man that looks at a woman lustfully has already committed adultery in his heart. This inward focus draws us to see the darkness in our own hearts.

Since men are visually stimulated in this way, when a woman presents herself with tight clothing to show off her figure or to reveal certain body parts and a man as a result lusts after her, she is guilty of being a partner in this sin of committing adultery in the heart.

While the focus may have been on the men's lustful looks in Paul and Jesus' age due to the level of clothing a woman wore, in this age the pendulum has swung back to the woman's field due to the vast array of immodesty.

Richard Baxter, 17th century Puritan pastor, writes in a Christian Directory about their clothing:

> To the ensnaring of the minds of the beholders in shameless, lustful, wanton passions, though you say, you intend it not, it is your sin, that you do that which probably will procure it, yea, that you did not your best to avoid it. And though it be their sin and vanity that is the cause, it is nevertheless your sin to be the unnecessary occasion: for you must consider that you live among diseased souls! And you must not lay a stumbling-block in their way, nor blow up the fire of their lust, nor make your ornaments their snares; but you must walk among sinful persons, as you would do with a candle among straw or gunpowder; or else you may see the flame which you would not foresee, when it is too late to quench it.

The way a woman dresses on the exterior is truly an expression of her heart. Sadly, in our day and age, women are careless and even thoughtless about what they wear. They follow the pattern of the world and the fashion of the world.

"Now we have received, not the spirit of the world, but the spirit which is of God; that we might know the things that are freely given to us of God." (1 Corinthians 2:12)

Today, clothing isn't even considered. To the modern person clothes have little to no moral value attached to them. A woman gets up in the morning, puts on her yoga pants and t-shirt and goes about her day, with no thought of how it might impact another human being or more importantly, what God thinks about it. We have not received the spirit of the world. Since that is the case we are not to follow the nature of the world when it comes to how we dress. The heart is the root of the problem: unconcerned about the word and will of God that brings forth these things.

A woman who dresses immodestly, though she may not be thinking of it, is asking for men to stare and lust after her. For most women this is not in their minds; they are not even desiring this; but they are unaware of the commands of God which are there to protect them. Many women who hear that God has standards in his Bible say, "That is someone else's problem, not mine. I am free to dress comfortably and as I please." Yes, of course you are; but we are not talking about your freedom. Our concern is what the Word of God commands. For a genuine believer in Christ, a woman is concerned about what Christ desires. As Richard Baxter wrote so adeptly, "... you must not lay a stumbling-block in their way, nor blow up the fire of their lust."

## Two Coverings

In the book of Genesis, we find that after Adam and Eve committed the original sin they felt shame and sought to cover their nakedness. This is the original form of clothing that sinful man used to clothe himself: "And the eyes of them both were opened, and they knew that they were naked; and they sewed fig leaves together, and made themselves aprons:" (Genesis 3:7). These aprons that Adam and Eve made to cover themselves are what we would call loin cloths and are basically as much covering as a bikini would offer. Notice, this is the clothing choice of the original sinners. This must have somehow given their consciences some reprieve. Then in verse 8 the LORD comes down to seek out Adam and Eve, then they hide themselves in the garden. God calls out to Adam and he responds "I was afraid, because I was naked." Even with the fig leaf bikini he determined he was still naked in the presence of God.

Afterward, God brought a curse upon the serpent, the woman and the earth. Then, God himself designs the clothes for Adam and Eve. "Unto Adam also and to his wife did the LORD God make coats of skins and clothed them: (Genesis 3:21). Adam and Eve chose clothing to merely cover their private parts. God brought forth an animal and killed it as a sin sacrifice for them. Then he took that and made it into what the bible calls "coats of skins." In other words, he made them clothing from the skin of the animal that was sacrificed for their sins. He clothed them with his sin offering for them. This is a perfect type of the New Testament: God clothes our inner man with our sin offering, we receive the Spirit of his Son, whereby we cry Abba, Father.

Looking more closely at the word "coats" in the Hebrew, the word is kûttôneth. It literally means to cover but was also a specific garment that was worn. The Brown Driver-Briggs Hebrew Lexicon states that kuttoneth means "a long shirt-like garment, usually of linen." The International Standard Bible Encyclopedia says, "Here. the "coat" (Hebrew kethōneth) was the ordinary inner garment worn by the Jew of the day, in which he did the work of the day (see Mat_24:18; Mar_13:16). It resembled the Roman tunic, corresponding most nearly to our long shirt, reaching below the knees always, and, in case it was designed for dress occasions, reaching almost to the ground."

God clothed Adam and Eve in a garment that truly covered their body. Clothing is meant to cover the body, not expose and reveal it. It is not meant to display every feature of the body, or emphasize the sexually attractive parts, but to literally cover up those parts. The kuttoneth was a shirt-like garment that covered from the neck down to below the knees. Effectively God condemns wearing so little clothes as a loin cloth or what we call a bikini. This was immodest dress that exposed their bodies more than what was acceptable. We can see that a modest dress would be something that covers the body from the neck to below the knees, not revealing the breasts or the thighs and not so tight that it is revealing everything.

## Christian Modesty

"Likewise, also women should adorn themselves in respectable apparel, with modesty and self-control, not with braided hair and gold or pearls or costly attire, but with what is proper for women who profess godliness—with good works." (1 Timothy 2:9-10)

Before closely examining this verse, I want to acknowledge that God has placed it into the heart of a woman to look beautiful for her husband. He did not make the woman to desire to be externally beautiful as the primary source of beauty and he does not purpose that a woman pursue external beauty to the extent that she lays aside the standards that God has set forth in his Word. A husband and wife, in the privacy of their own bedrooms, are free to "be naked and unashamed" because as Hebrews 13:4 says, "Marriage is honorable in all, and the bed undefiled ..." A casual perusal of the Song of Solomon demonstrates this truth.

In the aforementioned scripture, Paul is dealing with an external issue. The greater context of the verse is dealing with worship; but let's remember that our entire lives are to be lives of worship, not just in a church service. Women are commanded to wear modest clothing. Sisters in the Lord should wear clothes that clothe their body in a way that would not bring attention to their features. The word modest comes from the word moderate. An example would be: don't eat too little, but don't eat too much. Instead eat a moderate amount of food. Women should wear clothing that does not reveal too much, but they need not dress with a hijab covered from head to toe. Tight clothing that hugs the body or clothing that reveals the body too much should be avoided. It says her clothing should be chosen with "shamefacedness" and self-control. The word shamefacedness means bashfulness. To be bashful is to be a person that is shy, so choose your clothing in a way that shows that you are shy. Dressing in this way means that you do not want to show your body off, you want to conceal it and dissuade attention to yourself.

Paul says that women should wear modest apparel. I want to focus on the word apparel in the Greek language. The word apparel in English is a generic term for clothing. There is a generic term for clothing in Greek and that is himatismos, which is translated as attire near the end of I Timothy 2:10. However, the term that Paul uses here is katastole. The word katastole signifies a garment that would today be considered a dress. Here we have an important verse that tells us that the garment a sister in the Lord should wear is a dress and not pants. The phrase may also be translated "a modest long dress." There are some that challenge that katastole speaks of a long dress. In the next section I will go into greater detail on that point.

There are many women these days that wear clothes that reveal so much of their body that they are anything but shy. They want to show the whole world their body. This is a shame and should never happen in the life of a real believer. Sometimes the case is that a woman is not aware of how she is dressing and is just following the trends. Following the trends is no different than saying we are following the world. Instead of following trends we, as people that have given their lives to Christ, should dress according to the heart of Christ. These are not my words, but it is the teaching of Christ himself through his apostles.

When Paul mentions braided hair and gold and pearls, he is saying be balanced (modest) about it. It does not mean you cannot wear a necklace or braid your hair or wear expensive clothing but to be modest with everything you do in your dress.

There are Christians that say that the Bible does not speak about the clothes that we should wear, but only speaks about the heart. As you just read, Paul wrote about it and gave instructions to a pastor on what he should teach.

## Is Katastole Speaking of a Long Dress?

I was challenged by an ex-Message believer that my understanding of the term katastole is incorrect. He suggested I do additional research, which I have done. I have come to the same conclusion that the word katastole that Paul is using suggests a long garment down past the knees, what we refer to as a dress. Let's examine my research.

This was the singular reference I was given by the brother. I have provided quite a few more references that shed additional light on the term katastole that is translated as apparel in I Timothy 2:9. As you read you will see some Greek words that are impossible for non-Greek speakers to read. That is ok, just skip over them.

(s. Hippocr.; Mitt-Wilck. I/2, 12, 15 [88 B.C.] 'subjugation'; Is 61:3; EpArist, Joseph.) Like the verb?, the basic idea is keeping something in check, hence the use of this term in the sense of 'reserve, restraint' (IPriene 109, 186f [120 B.C.] and EpArist 284f: both texts w.; Epict. 2, 10, 15; 2, 21, 11: here personal deportment is certainly meant). The verb means to 'furnish, equip', a sense that extends itself to the putting on of garments. Hence katastole readily serves to express outward attire, either the character one exhibits in personal deportment or something to cover the body, namely attire, clothing (Jos., Bell. 2, 126; cp. Is 61:3; Plut., 154 [Pericl. 5, 1] also appears to be used in this sense) . dress in becoming manner (REB; dress modestly NRSV) 1 Ti 2:9.

The writer skillfully moves from the literal sense of garments to personal characteristics of 'modesty and self-control' as appropriate adornment. —DELG s.v. . M-M. TW. [5]

This is one lexicon of the Greek New Testament. They believe the word is used generally of the outward appearance. As in any lexical study (or study of the meaning of words in general) it serves us well to look at several sources.

This is from John Gill's commentary on I Timothy 2:9. Gill was the pastor that succeeded Charles Spurgeon at the Tabernacle in London. Gill writes:

**That women adorn themselves in modest apparel:** the word rendered 'apparel' signifies a long robe, which reaches down to the feet; and the word translated 'modes' signifies that which is clean, neat, and decent, yea, beautiful and ornamental; and the sense of the apostle is, that he would not have them to come to public worship in rags, and in dirty and filthy garments, but that their bodies should be covered with clean and decent raiment; so the Israelites washed their clothes that they might be ready to meet the Lord at Mount Sinai, Exo 19:14. The Jews always appeared in their best clothes on the sabbath day; this is one of their rules: (n).

Adam Clarke was a 19th century Methodist pastor and has a wonderful commentary on the Bible. Here are his comments regarding I Timothy 2:9:

**That women adorn themselves** – The apostle seems to refer here to different parts of the Grecian and Roman dress. The, stola, seems to have been originally very simple. It was a long piece of cloth, doubled in the middle, and

---

[5] William Arndt, Frederick W. Danker, and Walter Bauer, A Greek-English Lexicon of the New Testament and Other Early Christian Literature (Chicago: University of Chicago Press, 2000), 527.

sewed up on both sides, leaving room only for the arms; at the top, a piece was cut out, or a slit made, through which the head passed. It hung down to the feet, both before and behind, and was girded with the zona round the body, just under the breasts. It was sometimes made with, sometimes without, sleeves; and, that it might sit the better, it was gathered on each shoulder with a band or buckle. Some of the Greek women wore them open on each side, from the bottom up above the knee, so as to discover a part of the thigh. These were termed, showers (discoverers) of the thigh; but it was, in general, only young girls or immodest women who wore them thus.

The katastole seems to have been the same as the pallium or mantle, which, being made nearly in the form of the stola, hung down to the waist, both in back and front, was gathered on the shoulder with a band or buckle, had a hole or slit at top for the head to pass through, and hung loosely over the stola, without being confined by the zona or girdle. Representations of these dresses may be seen in Lens' Costume des Peuples de l'Antiquité, fig. 11, 12, 13, and 16. A more modest and becoming dress than the Grecian was never invented; it was, in a great measure, revived in England about the year 1805, and in it, simplicity, decency, and elegance were united; but it soon gave place to another mode, in which frippery and nonsense once more prevailed. It was too rational to last long; and too much like religious simplicity to be suffered in a land of shadows, and a world of painted outsides.

Adam Clarke is clearly describing a specific garment that is a modest long dress and not merely general external deportment. [6] The Jameson, Fausset, Brown Commentary states:

**In modest apparel** — 'in seemly guise' [Ellicott]. The adjective means properly. orderly, decorous, becoming; **_the_**

---

[6] a person's behavior or manners

*noun in secular writings means conduct, bearing. But here 'apparel.'* Women are apt to love fine dress; and at Ephesus the riches of some (1Ti_6:17) would lead them to dress luxuriously. The *Greek* in Tit_2:3 is a more general term meaning 'deportment.'

Here, the commentary is referring to how the word is used elsewhere, but in this instance, they acknowledge it is indeed a specific type of clothing, not a general term. They refer to the Greek word in Titus 2:3 as though it is quite the same word, however, it is a different word altogether, it only has the same root. In Titus 2:3 it is katastēma not katastole.

In the Theological Dictionary of the New Testament it states:

katastéll?, katastol?.

1) This verb means 'to put in its right place,' 'to arrange,' 'to restore order,' 'to pacify,' while the noun means 'propriety,' 'ordered conduct,' 'action with a view to such conduct,' and then 'clothing' (as a visible expression of decorum).

2) In the NT the verb occurs only in Acts 19:35–36, where the clerk calms the excited mob at Ephesus. The authority expressed by *katastéll?* differs from that expressed by the use of *katéseisen* when Paul as a witness to Christ brings the crowd to order at Jerusalem in Acts 21:27ff. The noun occurs in the advice to women believers in 1 Tim. 2:9, where Timothy is told to exhort them to adopt either a seemly demeanor or seemly apparel. *The context of worship perhaps supports the former rendering, but the use of stol? for 'garment' in the Apologists favors the latter.*

Here we see that there are various words that are connected together by their roots. However, at the end, they acknowledge that the Greek speaking Apologists (of the early church fathers) use the term in the sense of a specific type of garment.

### From the Bible Believers Commentary:

1 Timothy 2:9, Having discussed the personal requisites of the men who lead in public prayer, the apostle now turns to the things which should characterize **the women** who are in the congregation at such a time. First of all, he states that they should **adorn themselves in modest apparel, with propriety and moderation**. John Chrysostom gives a definition of modest apparel which can scarcely be improved upon:

And what then is *modest apparel?* Such as covers them completely and decently, and not with superfluous ornaments; for the one is decent and the other is not. What? Do you approach God to pray with broidered hair and ornaments of gold? Are you come to a ball? a marriage-feast? a carnival? There such costly things might have been seasonable: here not one of them is wanted. You have come to pray, to ask pardon for your sins, to plead for your offences, beseeching the Lord. ... Away with such hypocrisy!

John Chrysostom who lived from 347 to 407 A.D. and was an expert in the Greek languages.

Just because a version of the word is used in a certain way by secular authors does not mean that is the way the apostle is using the word. If you read John Chrysostom's notes about this verse he understood it to be modest apparel, not merely modest demeanor or behavior. He lived from 347 to 407 A.D. and he spoke Greek, which is the language the apostle wrote in, to Timothy.

If you notice, John Gill, Adam Clarke, Jameson and Faucet and Brown's commentaries you can see that indeed the apostle Paul did intend to communicate what I have written previously regarding the verse. We must delve deeper beyond the mere meanings of contemporary secular writings.

Before we conclude, let's examine closely the two words that make up the word katastole, kata means *gown* and stolay means a *gown or dress*. Therefore, we can conclude that Paul is expressing his teaching that women are to wear a modest dress and that both her dress and her character should be expressed with humility and sobriety.

## Distinction of the Sexes

"A woman shall not wear a man's garment, nor shall a man put on a woman's cloak, for whoever does these things is an abomination to the Lord your God." (Deuteronomy 22:5)

This verse is very simple and straightforward. A man should not wear women's clothes, a dress; and a woman should not wear man's clothes, pants. God wants a woman to dress like a woman and a man to dress like a man. Modern society has perverted this and made it normal for women to wear pants. The Word of God says a woman should not do so, and it is an abomination to God if she does it.

Oftentimes we are charged with focusing mostly on correcting the patterns of women's external appearance. The reason for this is that this has been the main target of Satan and he has perverted the proper morals of a woman to destroy morals in society.

It wasn't until the 20th Century that this Satanic process of taking away all societal norms of Christian dress took place. In the 19th Century and before, it was unthought of for a Christian woman to wear pants. This is expressed by the fact that in some places a woman would have been arrested for doing so. A woman that wore make-up was looked upon as a woman with "low morals" (ie-a prostitute).

During the time of this writing, women wore a specific

type of what we would refer to as a robe. Men also wore a specific type of garment that was for men, but we would also refer to it as a robe. If today a man's garment is pants and historically it was a specific manly robe, then does this not show that this is either cultural or a development of the time? In other words, if there is a standard and then that standard slowly develops over time, can't women now wear modest womanly pants since that is culturally acceptable? As men, we are not required to wear robes as our Lord Jesus would have done, but women are required to wear dresses. It seems like a double standard to some of modern ideology.

Let's examine this closely. Many times, reasoning departs from the Biblical text and never comes back to it. Deuteronomy 22:5 says that it is an abomination unto the LORD for a man to wear a woman's garment and a woman to wear a man's garment. It brings a confusion to the distinct maleness and femaleness that God created. He made them distinct and commands them to remain to so. Abomination means "abhorrence or disgust." This is not merely cultural or historical in nature. When it is disgusting to God then it remains disgusting to God.

Those that state a woman can wear women's pants are seeking to minimize or dismiss this verse. We cannot start from that point. God magnified it by attaching his abhorrence to the practice of cross dressing.

We can examine history and decide when men began to wear pants in various cultures; but we can actually go back to the very time that Jesus was on earth and even well before that and find that there were cultures where men wore pants. At the very same time, women did not wear pants. In some eastern cultures women wore pants underneath their dress, but not pants alone. As our western cultures developed, a woman always wore a dress or skirt. Men wore either a specific gown for a specific work they were a part of and in some instances wore pants. Women never have worn men's garments until the degrading of our culture. Let's examine the roots of pants for women in Western civilization.

## Roots of Pants in Western Civilization

In the early 1900's AD a *homosexual designer* in Paris began to make pants for women. This change in fashion was driven by the feminist movement in Victorian Europe. The women were expressing their rebellion against a patriarchal society, where a man operates in the role as the head of his home and as the head in society. Women were expressing the idea that they did not need a man and they no longer wanted to be under the authority of a man, as God intended and designated in scripture.

This is the origin of the widespread use of women wearing pants. It wasn't until the 1960's that designers started making blue jeans for women. It was not a normal thing for a woman to wear pants, but Satan, through lust and his desire to destroy society, has perverted this. Now, they call what is evil good and they call what is good evil. Women now wear pants that show every curve of their body, and they do it not knowing it's the spirit of this world causing them to express that they don't need to be under the authority which God designed. It's a shame! They say, "Who says that pants pertain to a man? Culture and times change." Yes, culture and times change, but the distinctions between the sexes do not. A woman in the attire of pants is wearing men's apparel. A feminine article of clothing is not pants, it is a dress or a skirt. A manly article of clothing is pants. This is just common sense and decency.

"For this is the love of God, that we keep his commandments. And his commandments are not burdensome." (1 John 5:3)

## Legalism?

I received a comment from a former Message believer that I wish to address. This comment was regarding modesty and pants. He is specifically referring to Deuteronomy 22:5.

I have seen Message women wearing dresses that were decidedly immodest and non-Message women wearing pants that were very modest. But those in the Message would condemn the woman in pants. Such legalism is not appropriate in the context of the New Testament church. – Former Message Believer

I also have seen Message believers wearing immodest clothing. They are following "the rule" of wearing a skirt or a dress. The problem is, that they are merely practicing specific restrictions. They are not practicing modesty. This is the point in the first place: they have not been taught that the root of the specific instruction is modesty.

Obedience to the scriptures is not legalism. How it is enforced, and the attitudes that go along, can be described as legalism. Pastors and believers can often be overzealous in their application of biblical commands, not using wisdom and applying the work of sanctification of the believers. We surely have a biblical standard to maintain in our church services, but we also give them time to learn and grow in their faith in the Word. God wants to sanctify and cleanse us from the inside out. Like the dove, that is cleansed by the oil that proceeds from within.

In Western culture, as we have shown, pants have their roots in the feminist movement and began to be marketed to general society because of several homosexual fashion designers in western Europe, particularly France. Much like the swimsuit industry in the United States, the designers of pants had a specific agenda they were seeking to perpetuate.

"But God be thanked, that ye were the servants of sin, but ye have obeyed from the heart that form of doctrine which was delivered you." Romans 6:17

The law is perfect and holy. But how it was enforced was not and how they treated others was legalistic. The law was ordained to give eternal life to man (Romans 7:10). The law is spiritual, and we are carnal, under sin, therefore that which was ordained to life led to death. The New Testament is to be delivered by the Spirit of God to our hearts. We obey the laws of God through the circumcision of the heart. Yet, it is quite clear that the apostles gave commands that God intended us to follow. As Paul wrote, we obeyed from our heart that form of doctrine which was delivered to us. The root of obedience, under the New Covenant, is the gift of the Holy Spirit, not external pressure and force. Instead, it is internal guidance and conviction from God, accompanied with a man of God feeding the flock of God, not beating the flock.

## Antinomianism?

Antinomian is a big word, but don't fear that. Many former Message believers and, for that matter, many Christians have become antinomian. Here is Webster's 1828 Dictionary definition of antinomian: "One of a sect who maintain that under the gospel dispensation, the law is of no use or obligation; or who hold doctrines which supersede the necessity of good works and a virtuous life. This sect originated with John Agricola about the year 1538."

Antinomian, "One of a sect who maintain that under the gospel dispensation, the law is of no use or obligation ..."

If we dismiss the law, we are dismissing the schoolmaster that is to lead us to Christ (Galatians 3:24-25). We dismiss that which is used to restrain sin and we dismiss part of the Word of God which we are to follow. The Spirit of God empowers and enables us to follow the moral law of God, and we know that the law is summed up in this: "You shall love your neighbor as yourself" Galatians 5:14. Once we come to faith in Christ, we are no longer under the schoolmaster. It does not mean the schoolmaster is no longer necessary or that we forget everything the schoolmaster said. It means we have graduated and now can put what we have learned from the schoolmaster into practice in our lives. Indeed, under grace, we are empowered and enabled by the Spirit of God to put it into practice.

Since we are under grace, this does not mean we can dismiss the law and state that it is now of no use. The law was laid down for ungodly and sinful people. That does not mean it was not made for the righteous person, instead it means that it is not directed against the godly man. It is for the godly man to follow by the fruit of the Spirit in his life. Under law it was by compulsion and under grace it is through the work of the Holy Spirit. The law is not dismissed.

"Now we know that the law is good if one uses it lawfully; understanding that the law is not laid down for the just but for the lawless and disobedient, for the ungodly and sinners, for the unholy and profane, for those who strike their fathers and mothers, for murderers, the sexually immoral, men who practice homosexuality, enslavers, liars, perjurers, and whatever else is contrary to sound doctrine." (I Timothy 2:8-10)

The law is not merely God's expression of his wrath against sin but is his eternal will for his people to follow.

It is not only the Ten Commandments that we are referring to when we speak of the law. There are many other moral commands attached to the law, outside of the commandments. Under the New Covenant, we cannot use the approach of the law to enforce them but rather we, by the Spirit of God, can discern biblical principles that we are to follow. Just because we are not under the law does not mean we dismiss the commands of God as being invalid for us. This is precisely how the apostle Paul used the Jewish scriptures (Old Testament) as he wrote, "For whatsoever things were written aforetime were written for our learning, that we through patience and comfort of the scriptures might have hope" (Romans 15:4)

In Paul's instructions to Timothy he writes regarding the scriptures that were in existence at that time, what we call the Old Testament: "All scripture is given by inspiration of God, and is profitable for doctrine, for reproof, for correction, for instruction in righteousness: That the man of God may be perfect, thoroughly furnished unto all good works" II Timothy 3:16-17. He instructs Timothy that the Old Testament (clearly the New Testament is considered in scriptures now) is profitable for doctrine (teaching), for evidence, for correction and for training in righteousness. Are we to then to dismiss the teachings, the evidences or proofs, the correction and training of the Old Testament? Obviously, we cannot.

When we refer to Deuteronomy 22:5 as a prohibition against women wearing pants and men wearing dresses, this is referred to as legalism. Remember, the Bible says what was written before was for our learning. So, we can refer to this scripture for our learning as a biblical principle. If you read the context of Deuteronomy 22, you see many moral commands given and then a few commands regarding clothing. Some of these are moral and some of them are ceremonial. We can look to all of them for our learning, for spiritual types, and sometimes as prophetic passages. Paul used the scripture: "You shall not muzzle the ox while he is threshing," as a command to give an offering to a minister of the gospel.

Using Deuteronomy 22:5 as an example or as a teaching for us to follow is well within the normative use of the Old Testament. It is not a reference to legalism: it is a teaching. Like any other teaching from the Bible, under the New Covenant, it is to be obeyed from the heart through the Spirit of God.

29

## Common Decency

When we go to work for a company, they have a dress code. The dress code pertains to modesty and professionalism. This is a normal practice the world over, and no one questions it. Yet, when it comes to the Christian faith, the modern church rejects the idea that God would want us to surrender our will to the point that we would dress the way he desires. When we submit to God regarding not having sex before marriage, it is not considered legalism, it is considered obedience and that obedience protects us and preserves us for our future spouse and for the glory of God. When God commands us to dress modestly and wear clothing that pertains to our manhood or womanhood it is to reflect the character of Christ.

# Chapter 3

# MAKE-UP

Is make-up approved or allowed by Scripture? To properly understand this subject, I want to start by examining the motive of the heart. This is where sinful behavior comes from, so let's first discern the motive. While many are simply following the spirit of this world and conforming to cultural norms without determining motive, let us observe what is behind the "cultural norm."

Is it possible that the motivation for wearing make-up is modesty and the glory of God? The purpose of make-up is external beauty: it can be to cover up blemishes or to brighten the lips, lengthen the lashes, or whatever the external effect is that you want to produce. The motivation for wearing make-up is clearly not modesty or to draw attention to a woman's character. Its motive is merely outward beauty. Make-up is putting something on that you are not. Hence a woman often says, "I need to put on my face." The definition of "put on" is a deception or hoax. This is clearly what is behind make-up. It is a hoax. The woman does not look like that at all, but to look more beautiful she devises a hoax using various paints and powders. But is this how God wants a woman to behave? I say behave because make-up is not a given, it is a behavior that is chosen, and it is chosen because that is the "spirit of this world." In fact, scripture does not speak highly of its usage. It is mentioned at least three times in scripture and never in a positive manner. This excerpt comes from the book "Strange Scriptures to The Western Mind:"

Painting does not appear to have been by any means universal among the Hebrews. References to it are few; and in each instance it seems to have been unworthy of a woman of high character. Thus Jezebel, 'put her eyes in painting' (2 Kings 9:30). Jeremiah says of the harlot city, 'though thou rentest thy face with painting' (Jeremiah 4:30). And Ezekiel again makes it a characteristic of a harlot (Ezekiel 23:40).

Jezebel brought idolatry to the forefront in Israel; she caused her husband Ahab to slip further into wickedness and idol worship. In 2 Kings 9:30 Ahab is dead and Jehu has been ordained of God to bring his wrath upon the house of Ahab. Jezebel learns of this and she decides to take matters into her own hands. She put make-up on her eyes and puts on her crown and then goes to stand in the window. Though she was a grandmother at the time her purpose was to declare her pride of station and to seduce Jehu (who was also an older man) into marrying her and thus protecting her life. Then shortly after that she was thrown from the balcony of her home, and dogs came to feed on her dead body. That certainly isn't a positive picture. Here make-up is mentioned in regard to pride and seduction. Let's review other scriptures that reference this phenomenon:

"And when thou art spoiled, what wilt thou do? Though thou clothest thyself with crimson, though thou deckest thee with ornaments of gold, though thou rentest thy face with painting, in vain shalt thou make thyself fair; thy lovers will despise thee, they will seek thy life." (Jeremiah 4:30)

Jeremiah was a prophet to the kingdom of Judah. He had been prophesying of the destruction and captivity of the people. He has spoken of the children of Judah as dressing herself seductively purposely to get assistance from the neighboring states. This is the practice of prostitutes to seduce men to commit fornication. When he wants to describe a whore, he speaks of decking herself with ornaments, that is, putting on a lavish amount of jewelry, a head dress, etc. Then he says "... thou rentest thy face with painting." Another way to put this would be the way the ESV translates it, "... that you enlarge your eyes with paint?" So, according to the word of the Lord a woman that paints her face is identified with a prostitute: Ezekiel 23:40 "They even sent for men to come from afar, to whom a messenger was sent; and behold, they came. For them you bathed yourself, painted your eyes, and adorned yourself with ornaments."

Ezekiel is prophesying about the wickedness of the northern kingdom of 10 tribes and the southern kingdom of Judah. He is saying that instead of turning to the LORD for your help you went through this tremendous process of adorning yourself in order to seduce the other nations around you to help. In verse 43 Ezekiel writes that she is "... worn out by adultery, now they will continue to use her for a whore." Then in verse 44 he calls them prostitutes and lewd women. In 45 he writes that a sentence will be passed against them, that they are adulteresses. Once again, the LORD identifies painting the eyes with being an ungodly woman, a prostitute. This is God's viewpoint toward the use of make-up; you are painting yourself up like a prostitute. Now, as I stated before, most women are completely unaware of this and perhaps become offended by this statement. You were once in ignorance to this and of course now you are not. It is important that you take time to pray and consider closely what has been written.

The Scripture says, "Abstain from all appearance of evil," (1 Thessalonians 5:22). The Bible connects the use of make-up with idolatry and immorality. Wearing make-up is an immodest thing that draws the attention to outward beauty instead of the inner character of the heart. Why are you wearing make-up? Examine your heart.

Make-up dates back thousands of years in pagan societies. Certainly, the Jewish people were negatively influenced by pagan ethnic groups that surrounded them, as we read in the Old Testament. However, it became more prevalent in modern society in the early 20th Century because of the entertainment world and Hollywood. [7]

## Did Queen Esther Wear Make-Up?

I have heard of a few people mention that Queen Esther wore make-up. I want to examine this charge against her to see if the Bible reveals whether or not this is so. Let's examine the Scriptures that some individuals have used to "prove" that she wore make-up. First, I will give you each reference in the King James Version and then in the English Standard Version. After we do that let's look at the original language and find out what the words actually mean.

### Cosmetics vs. Things for Purification

KJV     (Esther 2:3)
        And let the king appoint officers in all the provinces of his kingdom, that they may gather together all the fair young virgins unto Shushan the palace, to the house of the women, unto the custody of Hege the king's chamberlain, keeper of the women; and let their *things for purification* be given them:

ESV     (Esther 2:3)
        And let the king appoint officers in all the provinces of his kingdom to gather all the beautiful young virgins to the harem in Susa the capital, under custody of Hegai, the king's eunuch, who is in charge of the women. Let their *cosmetics* be given them.

---

[7] http://en.wikipedia.org/wiki/History_of_cosmetics

KJV    (Esther 2:9)
And the maiden pleased him, and she obtained kindness of him; and he speedily gave her her ***things for purification***, with such things as belonged to her, and seven maidens, which were meet to be given her, out of the king's house: and he preferred her and her maids unto the best place of the house of the women.

ESV    (Esther 2:9)
And the young woman pleased him and won his favor. And he quickly provided her with her ***cosmetics*** and her portion of food, and with seven chosen young women from the king's palace and advanced her and her young women to the best place in the harem.

KJV    (Esther 2:12)
Now when every maid's turn was come to go in to king Ahasuerus, after that she had been twelve months, according to the manner of the women, (for so were the days of their ***purifications*** accomplished, to wit, six months with oil of myrrh, and six months with sweet odours, and with other things for the purifying of the women;)

ESV    (Esther 2:12)
Now when the turn came for each young woman to go in to King Ahasuerus, after being twelve months under the regulations for the women, since this was the regular period of their ***beautifying***, six months with oil of myrrh and six months with spices and ointments for women.

## Examining the Hebrew

Verses 3 and 9 both have the same Hebrew word that is

translated as cosmetics in the ESV and purification in the KJV. The word in Hebrew is "tamruq" and from Strong's Dictionary it states: "properly a *scouring*, that is, *soap or perfumery* for the bath; figuratively a *detergent*: – X cleanse, (thing for) purification (-fying)." So, the purpose of the application of "cosmetics" (ESV) was to purify or cleanse. This quote cosmetic un-quote that was used was not make-up, instead its purpose was to purify or cleanse the body. The King James translators chose, "things for purification" based upon the literal meaning of the Hebrew word tamruq, since it literally means "a scouring."

The ESV translators chose the word "cosmetics." This leads some people to believe that Esther put on make-up at this time. If you read, Esther verse 12, note the cosmetics that were applied to her were "oil of myrrh and ... spices and ointments for women." Next, if we examine the word "cosmetics" we can see that though the ESV translators chose a somewhat confusing word they are technically correct. The word cosmetics according to Webster's Dictionary: "**COSMETIC**: a. s as z. [Gr., order, beauty.] Beautifying; improving beauty, particularly the beauty of the skin. **COSMETIC**, n. Any preparation that renders the skin soft, pure and white, and helps to beautify and improve the complexion."

According to the actual meaning of cosmetics we can see that indeed oil of myrrh, spices and ointments are cosmetics; but they are not the painting of the eyes as was the characteristic of heathen women in biblical times.

We can confidently conclude that these verses do not at all teach us that Esther wore make-up. She went through a purification or cleansing process for one year in to be made ready for her husband, the King. That purification process was done with bathing and the application of oil of myrrh, spices and ointments. She was not "purified" with make-up or with painting of her eyes. This does not fit the context of the scripture at all. Those who are using this as proof that wearing make-up is scripturally acceptable are twisting the meaning of cosmetics and the context of the scriptures themselves.

The book of Esther does not tell us that she did not wear make-up, but it also does not tell us that she did. Remember, Queen Esther is not necessarily a great example for us. She hid her Jewish heritage from the King, she married a pagan, the Babylonian captivity was over and she could have returned to Israel, but she chose to stay behind and since she hid her heritage she was likely eating meats forbidden by Mosaic Law. But not only that, at first, she refused to help the Jews because she was scared for her own life. She made the right choice in the end, but she is not necessarily the model of Christian life that we want to follow, whether she wore make-up or not.

## Make-up in the US and Europe

During the early years of the 20th century, make-up became fashionable in the United States of America and Europe, owing to the influence of ballet and theatre stars such as Mathilde Kschessinska and Sarah Bernhardt. But the most influential new development of all was the movie industry in Hollywood. Among those who saw the opportunity for mass-market cosmetics were Max Factor Sr., Elizabeth Arden and Helena Rubinstein.

Do we want to follow Hollywood, or do we want to follow the word of God? Hollywood glorifies outward beauty and destroys the soul; but God points to inward character and the beauty of holiness. Is modern fashion your absolute or is the Word of God your absolute?

## Why Focus on Outward Appearance?

While in Islamic culture they go to one end of the spectrum, in the West they go to the other end of the spectrum. In Islam a code of ethics is enforced, often with the threat of punishment. In the West there is no code of ethics at all: anything goes. Women walk around with absolutely no modesty: showing off their body, painting their faces, wearing tight clothes, and in some cases barely any clothes at all. God calls us to modesty according to the scriptures.

Remember the High priest? He was given certain requirements for his clothing, his hair, and his appearance. In Zechariah 3:1-7, when Joshua the High priest was in the presence of God he had to put on clean garments. He had to put on clothes that were pleasing to God. We are not following Old Testament Law, but we follow the same God that gave us these biblical standards to follow.

## Adornment of the Inner Man Vs. Outward Man

"Whose adorning let it not be that outward adorning of plaiting the hair, and of wearing of gold, or of putting on of apparel. But let it be the hidden man of the heart, in that which is not corruptible, even the ornament of a meek and quiet spirit, which is in the sight of God of great price." (1 Peter 3:3-4)

God's focus is on the beauty of holiness, the inner man, and the character and conduct thereof. Peter says, adorn yourself not with elaborate braids, wearing gold or expensive clothes, but let it be the hidden man of the heart, a meek and quiet spirit. You can wear braids, gold and clothes, but don't spend most of your time focusing on your appearance. Focus on your heart and your attitude: that is what is beautiful in God's eyes. From this inner beauty of holiness and godly character, adorn yourself with modest dress.

## Is it Modest?

The Bible commands modesty; therefore, we must ask the question, is make-up modest?

"Ye are our epistle written in our hearts, known and read of all men." (2 Corinthians 3:2)

We as believers are a letter that is read by everyone that sees us. That speaks of both our love and behavior towards others, but also our appearance. Our appearance with our hair, jewelry, make-up and clothing impact the letter that people are reading as they watch our lives.

"Let your moderation be known unto all men. The Lord is at hand." (Philippians 4:5)

The word "moderation" is quite an encompassing word. It speaks of modesty, but also of humility, kindness, gentleness, care, concern, mildness, etc. It connotes both, our behavior and our appearance. As we have shown through the Scriptures, there is an emphasis on godly external appearance.

So, going back to the title of this section, the Bible commands modesty and, therefore, we ask the question, is make-up modest or immodest? It might seem like an absurd question to some, but we should judge all things according to the scriptures. Notice what the Encyclopedia Americana states, in 1956, regarding make-up:

"The last two decades have seen make-up progress from its early category of woman's conceit to become an art and an integral part of feminine beauty and psychology. Chief credit for this about face in the acceptance of widespread use of cosmetics should go to the motion picture industry, which set new standards of beauty and...brought new products and principles of application and use to the world's women." [8]

Historically make-up was looked at as an item of vanity

[8] Encyclopedia Americana, Vol. 18, 1956 Edit., p. 157

and not something a godly woman would adorn. Notice, what the scriptures state about vanity:

"Behold, thou hast made my days as an handbreadth; and mine age is as nothing before thee: verily every man at his best state is altogether vanity. Selah. Surely every man walketh in a vain shew: surely they are disquieted in vain: he heapeth up riches, and knoweth not who shall gather them." (Psalms 39:5-6)

# Jezebel

We've already given a basic overview of the subject of Jezebel, but before we move on to the next chapter let's review the scriptures and the life of Jezebel in greater detail. In the books of 1st and 2nd Kings, we learn of a woman named Jezebel. She was a Sidonian (non-Israelite) and the daughter of their king. She was married to Ahab and brought Baal worship with her. She was a fanatical worshipper of Baal. She had over 400 prophets of Baal that were employed by her. She used Ahab's authority to murder and steal the land of Naboth so Ahab would own the vineyard. Ahab was killed in battle and her son Ahaziah became king of the 10 tribes of Israel. Then, Ahaziah's brother, Jehoram (or Joram), reigned over Israel. Jezebel remained as an occupant of the palace and exerted authority as the dowager Queen Mother.

Elisha, led by the LORD, was instructed to anoint Jehu (an Israeli military commander) king of Israel and to commission him to destroy the house of Ahab. Elisha sent one of his servants to go and fulfill this task. Immediately, Jehu conspired to kill King Joram. He went to Jezreel where Joram was recovering from his injuries in the war against Syria. The king of Judah went to visit him there as he recovered. As they learned that Jehu was coming to them they prepared their chariots to go out to meet him. They asked him, "Is it peace Jehu" and he answered, "What peace can there be, so long as the whorings and the sorceries of your mother Jezebel are so many:" 2 Kings 9:22. The two kings turned and fled in different directions. Jehu took his bow and arrow and shot Joram. Then he pursued the king of Judah and killed him as well.

Jezebel heard that Jehu killed her son and made a last effort to save herself. "When Jehu came to Jezreel, Jezebel heard of it. And she painted her eyes and adorned her head and looked out of the window:" 2 Kings 9:30. In the KJV it says that she painted her face; but a more precise translation would be that she painted her eyes as is noted in the ESV. The KJV also says that she tired her head. This sounds a little mysterious, but, basically, it means that she beautified her hair. We could spend much time on oriental traditions of the time, but we could simply say she did her hair for a special event. She prepared herself in all her royal attire and it is recorded that after the event Jehu ate dinner. So perhaps she prepared herself in royal clothing and prepared an official meal of state for Jehu's arrival.

Instead of mourning the loss of her son she went to win the favor of the person that assassinated him. So, then, what was the reason that Jezebel painted her eyes?

There are at least two possible reasons. One, is that she sought to seduce and become the wife of Jehu. The reason for this viewpoint is consistent with her reputation later in the Bible as a seducer. In Revelation 2:20 it says: "But I have this against you, that you tolerate that woman Jezebel, who calls herself a prophetess and is teaching and seducing my servants to practice sexual immorality and to eat food sacrificed to idols." She is both teaching and seducing God's servants to practice sexual immorality. One objection against this viewpoint is that she was an older woman: mother of a king who was in his 20's. However, if we read closely the recounting of Jehu, we realize that he was a servant of King Ahab in his protective guard. This is not something a small child would be doing. It would take a man that has proven himself and risen in the ranks of the military to get to that position. Then having served Ahab he served Ahazaiah and Joram. Jehu himself was not young, but a man who had experienced a career in the military. After his ascent to the throne he ruled for 28 years. It is not known exactly how old Jehu was, but he was certainly not too far removed from the age of Jezebel. The next problem with this viewpoint are her words upon Jehu's arrival, which were, "Is it peace, you Zimri, murderer of your master?" He is referred to as Zimri because he was a man that killed King Elah of Israel and Zimri was king for a very short time and had a terrible end of his life by running into the palace that was set on fire. Her tone is one of defiance. You have killed your master and your end will be like that of Zimri, overthrow of your government and suicide. If she wanted to become the wife of Jehu she would greet him differently than this.

The second viewpoint is, as the Queen Mother she was simply trying to appear in the grandeur of her office and to show she was not giving it up in shame. She was, with pride and arrogance, saying I was born a royal and I will die a royal. She was not putting on make-up and getting dressed in royal attire to seduce Jehu. She was in one last act of defiance showing that she was the royal authority.

Even though the Bible refers to her as a seducer and she adorned herself in royal clothes and painted her face her intention was not to seduce or to win the affections of Jehu. Her greeting to Jehu shows what was in her heart; she was defying him and showing that she was the royal authority. Perhaps it was her fanatical belief in Baal that led her to view herself as the prophetess and protector of Baal worship. She was defiant to the last moment of her life to prove her faithfulness to Baal and her royal authority. We do not know all of her motivations, but it is clear she was dressing herself to show her royal authority and defy Jehu.

*Painting of the eyes or wearing of make-up is not connected to godliness or godly women.*

## Tired Her Hair

"And when Jehu was come to Jezreel, Jezebel heard of it; and she painted her face, and tired her head, and looked out at a window." (2 Kings 9:30)

We often condemn Jezebel for "painting her face", but we leave out the last part that was mentioned in the same breath and that is she, "tired her head." That is, she adorned her head. Notice it does not say she put her hair up in braids or anything to that effect. It says that she "adorned" her head. It was the custom of royalty and priestesses to wear elaborate headdresses to express their exalted and proud position.

Notice, it was not that she braided her hair that was spoken of, rather, she put on a headdress, much like what you see pictured here in the movie Cleopatra. To use a parallel, the Queen of England does not dress in her full royal apparel every day. Normally she dresses like the picture on the left below, but on special occasions of state she dresses as the picture on the right.

Jezebel adorned herself for a special occasion and dressed as a Queen in royal splendor to show her rank and position. This painting of the eyes and wearing of an

elaborate headdress is not becoming for a woman of godly character. Rather, it speaks of pride and vanity, nothing a Christian woman would desire to be characterized by.

### Earrings

In Ezekiel 16:12 it speaks of God clothing his Bride, the nation of Israel: "And I put a jewel on thy forehead, and earrings in thine ears, and a beautiful crown upon thine head." This, of course, is a spiritual type of him clothing them with righteousness and ears to hear the truth. We can read that wealthy women in the East wore these types of adornments on a regular basis: Genesis 24:22, Genesis 24:42; Exodus 32:2; Job 42:11; Proverbs 11:22; Isaiah 3:21; Hosea 2:13. Though this was the normal attire for that time, does not mean that it is necessarily a recommended or allowed form of adornment. Let's notice what Jacob commands to his family—this is after the time that Abraham's servant gave earrings to Rachel (Jacob's mother) for her engagement gift:

"God said to Jacob, 'Arise, go up to Bethel and dwell there. Make an altar there to the God who appeared to you when you fled from your brother Esau.' So, Jacob said to his household and to all who were with him, 'Put away the foreign gods that are among you and purify yourselves and change your garments. Then let us arise and go up to Bethel, so that I may make there an altar to the God who answered me in the day of my distress and has been with me wherever I have gone.' They gave to Jacob all the foreign gods that they had, and the rings that were in their ears. Jacob hid them under the terebinth tree that was near Shechem." (Genesis 35:1-4)

This Scripture describes how Jacob cleansed his household of idolatry. The people were told to bring him all their foreign gods and the rings in their ears. The people took their earrings out and gave them to Jacob and he buried them. Earrings and idolatry are directly connected. The people often wore amulets on their earrings showing they belonged to and were seeking the blessing of, false gods. Earrings and nose rings are not encouraged in the culture of the Bible: they are connected to idolatry. And idolatry is connected to evil spirits.

Chapter 4

# LONG HAIR

"Every man praying or prophesying, having his head covered, dishonoureth his head. But every woman that prayeth or prophesieth with her head uncovered dishonoureth her head: for that is even all one as if she were shaven. For if the woman be not covered, let her also be shorn: but if it be a shame for a woman to be shorn or shaven, let her be covered. For a man indeed ought not to cover his head, forasmuch as he is the image and glory of God: but the woman is the glory of the man. For this cause ought the woman to have power on her head because of the angels. Judge in yourselves: is it comely that a woman pray unto God uncovered? Doth not even nature itself teach you that if a man have long hair, it is a shame unto him? But if a woman have long hair, it is a glory to her: for her hair is given her for a covering. But if any man seem to be contentious, we have no such custom, neither the churches of God." (1 Corinthians 11:4-7, 10, 13-16)

## Common Concerns regarding long hair

Some people seek to state this is a cultural issue only and that in the 21st Century we don't have to follow this. However, I want to start by listing four points that reveal this is not merely cultural.

1)    Paul references the headship of man. This is not a

cultural issue, it is an eternal truth.

2) Paul states this should be done "because of the angels" - there is no cultural boundary to angels.

3) Paul states that the churches of God have only one custom. That is, all the churches throughout the world have this custom. There is not one custom in Macedonia, another in Asia, and another in Israel. There is only one custom (or practice) for the church. It does not vary by culture.

4) The Roman empire spanned many different cultures during Paul's time. He did not single out any as being excepted from this natural law.

Paul is talking about two things. One, the normal customs of the time and two, eternal truth. Firstly, he speaks of a veil or a covering that was common for women to wear in his time. They covered their hair with a veil for the sake of showing modesty. This was done throughout the Roman and Middle Eastern world at the time. The Corinthian women rejected this idea and Paul asked that it be continued. Wearing a veil was a cultural means of displaying that a woman was under the authority of her husband. This is no longer the practice of our time.

There is an eternal truth here and that is the distinction between sexes regarding hair. He references headship of man, angelic beings, and nature. A man should have short hair and a woman should have long hair. This is not merely a human custom, but this is an important distinction that God makes between man and woman. The Word of God says it is a shameful thing for a woman to have short hair.

The word used for covering is a "veil." Paul writes that a woman should wear a veil while praying or prophesying. Then he makes this statement that reveals what kind of veil he is referencing: "... her hair is given her for a covering." In other words, her hair is given to her to be her veil. Whether a scarf is worn or not is irrelevant. God tells us a woman's hair was given to her as her veil. This is a natural thing that God gave from the beginning of time, a woman's long hair and a man's short hair. The Bible says a woman's long hair is her glory.

During the time of Paul's writing, there were two reasons a woman would cut her hair: one, if her husband died and she was in mourning; and the next would be if it was done forcibly as a punishment for prostitution. According to the Bible it is a shameful thing for a woman to cut her hair and if she does it, it is the same as though she were dishonoring her head, her husband.

A man with long hair is doing something shameful and humiliating himself; but a woman with long hair is showing the honor of her womanhood. Sisters keep your hair long, don't cut it or trim it, just let it grow.

In the times of mourning for the loss of her husband a woman would cut off her hair. The women desired to avoid this custom and to show they were still mourning their husband they simply trimmed the ends of their hair. It is not a normal thing for a woman to cut her hair at all. She is to let it grow according to the teaching of the Bible. And a man should have short hair to show he is honoring his head, Jesus Christ. A man with long hair is dishonoring Christ according to the Bible.

## How did short hair on women become acceptable?

Leading up to the early 20th Century, i.e. 1900's, it was not at all acceptable or normal for a woman to cut her hair. Waist length hair was not at all uncommon among women and in fact cutting a woman's hair at all was something only done in cases of extreme necessity, that is, when a woman was sick. [9] It was in 1908 that a high fashion designer named

Paul Poiret of Paris, France chopped his model's hair for a fashion show. In France, this hairstyle was called "mode a la garconne" which means, the hairstyle of a man. In American English it was called "the bob" and it was viewed as a boy's haircut. In 1917, many fashionable women began to "bob" their hair and it represented the new American woman, who was free from the old fashioned social norms. This was also directly connected to feminism.

We basically have all of human history that a woman has had long, uncut hair. Then, in the 20th Century, an assault on God's order starts in the form of throwing off the old biblical norms. Now Satan has brought these biblical truths to a place of scorn, rejection and unimportance.

Sometimes our sisters in Christ feel that it is unimportant whether or not her hair is long. The question becomes a confusion about how Paul wrote of the veil and of long hair. As we examine the subject, Paul concludes that a woman's hair is given to her as her veil and it is shameful for her to have short hair. We can clearly see according to the Bible that a woman should have long hair. This is very clear and simple to understand. The question that always follows is, "how long, is long hair?" Long hair is, as long as God allows it to be when it is uncut. We find in the Old Testament that a man or woman under a Nazirite vow was to allow their hair to grow and never let a razor or scissors touch it. Therefore, a woman should simply allow her hair to grow as long as God makes it. The length may vary greatly between women, depending on the health of their hair and genetics, diet and the part of the world you live in.

---

[9] Tradition in Action

http://www.traditioninaction.org/Questions/F064_ShortHair.htm

# CONCLUSION

Jesus said if you love me keep my words. The words of Jesus are what we read in the Scripture, not merely select portions of the Gospels, and his commands are not to be burdensome. They are to protect us and preserve us so that we can truly manifest the character of Jesus Christ.

"There is no fear in love; but perfect love casteth out fear: because fear hath torment. He that feareth is not made perfect in love." (1 John 4:18)

*These are not words of fear to control your life. They are words of God to preserve your character and bring honor and glory to God.*

The 20th Century started with an intense demonic assault on the Christian foundation of purity and modesty. It came through fashion designers and Hollywood. As Spirit-filled Christians I hope you can see this tactic of the devil that has led to all the perversions of society that we see today. He started his attack using feminism, Hollywood and fashion designers. This, then went into mass media and slowly became the norm of society. But this norm of society was once thought to be a great perversion among Christians. Now, it is the norm for Christians. I submit, that the Church of the living God should not be conformed to this world but be transformed by the renewing of their mind (Read Romans 12:1-2). This world's fashions are perverted according to the lusts of the devil. As Spirit-filled believers we base our outward appearance on the Word of God not the word of Hollywood. What will you choose? The Word or Hollywood?

We see the sexual perversion of Hollywood laid bare today. Now, everyone is aware of the sex for work, rape, sexual assault and pedophilic culture of Hollywood. This began with the push for women to have a man's haircut, wear men's clothes and have the authority of men. This total perversion of what is right is Satan's main agenda for this day. He created his own version of Eden, where perversion rules the day.

I ask one thing of you, brothers and sisters: pray about what you have read. Search the scriptures and pray earnestly, asking God what he would have you to do about what you read. If you are not filled with the Spirit, then it is important that you first get filled with the Spirit. When you are filled with the Spirit, you can know the Spirit of truth guiding you into all truth (John 16:13).

Made in the USA
Monee, IL
22 December 2023

48114435R00038